I Am LATINO

The Beauty in Me

Sandra L. Pinkney photographs by Myles C. Pinkney

LITTLE, BROWN AND COMPANY
New York · Boston

To my parents, Frances Louise and Alfred, who taught me to sense the beauty.
—S.P.

To the children of Head Start in Newburgh, each one of you is beautiful.
—M.P.

Also by Sandra and Myles Pinkney:

Shades of Black

A Rainbow All Around Me

Little, Brown and Company · Hachette Book Group USA · 1271 Avenue of the Americas, New York, NY 10020
Visit our Web site at www.lb-kids.com

First Edition: July 2007

Pinkney, Sandra L.
Sense the beauty / by Sandra Pinkney ; photographs by Myles Pinkney.—1st ed.
p. cm.
Summary: Photographs and poetic text celebrate the beauty and diversity of Latino children.
ISBN-13: 978-0-316-16009-4 (hardcover)
ISBN-10: 0-316-16009-1 (hardcover)
1. Latin Americans—Juvenile fiction. [1. Latin Americans—Fiction.]
I. Pinkney, Myles C., ill. II. Title.
PZ7.P63348Sen 2007
[E]—dc22   2006001164
10 9 8 7 6 5 4 3 2 1
SC   Printed in China

Use your senses
and you will see,
there is beauty
in everything.

I am Latina.
Can you sense the beauty?

listen

to the melody in my language

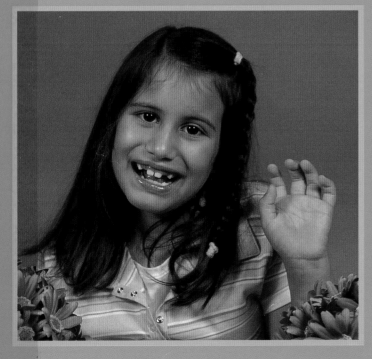

Buenos días (Good morning)

¿Cómo está? (How are you?)
Muy bien (Very good)

Hasta luego (See you later)

Adiós (Good-bye)

I am Latino.
Can you sense the beauty?

feel
my music explode

Foot-gliding Tango

Body-swaying Baladas

Hip-swinging Salsa

Finger-snapping Flamenco

I am Latina.
Can you sense the beauty?

see

the love in my family (mi familia)

Strong Papa

Caring Mama

Loving Abuelita (Grandmother)

Playful Hermano (Brother)

Happy Hermana (Sister)

I am Latino.
Can you sense the beauty?

smell and taste my foods

Thick, rich

Batido de plátano (banana milk shake)

Lip-smacking
Pica pollo (fried chicken)

Scrumptious Tostones

Delicious Empanadas

Mouthwatering Tamales

Use your senses

You will see Beauty—Magnificently

I am Latino. I am the Beauty!!!